THE CROWD YOU'RE IN WITH

THE CROWD
YOU'RE IN WITH

⊰A PLAY⊱

REBECCA GILMAN

NORTHWESTERN UNIVERSITY PRESS

EVANSTON, ILLINOIS

Northwestern University Press
www.nupress.northwestern.edu

Printed in the United States of America

10 9 8 7 6 5 4 3 2

LIBRARY OF CONGRESS
CATALOGING-IN-PUBLICATION DATA

Gilman, Rebecca Claire.
    The crowd you're in with : a play /
Rebecca Gilman.
        p. cm.
    "The Crowd You're In With premiered
at the Magic Theatre in San Francisco
on November 17, 2007, with Chris
Smith as artistic director; David Jobin,
managing director; Amy Glazer, director
. . . [and] was subsequently produced
by the Goodman Theatre in Chicago
on June 1, 2009. It was directed by
Wendy C. Goldberg."
    ISBN 978-0-8101-2644-2 (pbk. :
alk. paper) 1. Parenthood—Decision
making—Drama. 2. Childlessness—
Decision making—Drama. I. Title.
PS3557.I456C76 2009
812'.54—dc22

                                    2009019637

CONTENTS

PRODUCTION HISTORY

The Crowd You're In With premiered at the Magic Theatre in San Francisco on November 17, 2007, with Chris Smith as artistic director; David Jobin, managing director; Amy Glazer, director; set designer, Erik Flatmo; lighting designer, Kurt Landisman; costume designer, Meg Neville; sound designer, Sara Huddleston; stage manager, Angela Nostrand; and assistant director, Scott Walecka. The cast was as follows:

Dan . . . . Kevin Rolston
Jasper . . . . T. Edward Webster
Melinda . . . . Makela Spielman
Windsong . . . . Allison Jean White
Tom . . . . Charles Shaw Robinson
Karen . . . . Lorri Holt
Dwight . . . . Chris Yule

The Crowd You're In With was subsequently produced by the Goodman Theatre in Chicago beginning on June 1, 2009. It was directed by Wendy C. Goldberg. Sets were designed by Kevin Depinet, lighting by Josh Epstein, sound by Josh Horvath, and costumes by Rachel Healy. The stage manager was Kimberly Osgood.

The cast was as follows:

Dan . . . . Kiff Vanden Heuvel
Jasper . . . . Coburn Goss
Melinda . . . . Janelle Snow
Windsong . . . . Stephanie Childers
Tom . . . . Rob Riley
Karen . . . . Linda Gehringer
Dwight . . . . Sean Cooper

The Crowd You're In With was developed at The Eugene O'Neill National Playwrights Conference (Wendy C. Goldberg, artistic director).

A very special thanks to Amy Glazer, Wendy Goldberg, Susan Booth, Robert Falls, Ed Sobel, Tanya Palmer, and George Lane, for all their support and guidance. Thank you to the city of Chicago for the inspiration. And, as always, love and thank you to Charles for everything.

THE CROWD YOU'RE IN WITH

CHARACTERS

Dan, early thirties

Jasper, early thirties

Melinda, early thirties

Windsong, early thirties

Tom, late fifties

Karen, late fifties

Dwight, thirtyish

[*At rise, the backyard of a two-flat on the north side of Chicago. There is a fence, a nice little garden, a table and chairs. A gate in the fence leads into the alley. The back door and porch of the first-floor unit are visible, as are a set of outside stairs leading up to the second-floor unit. On the back porches are flower boxes. All is well maintained, homey. There is a gas grill, and next to it is a washtub filled with ice and beers. A boom box and CDs sit on a small table. Outdoor lights are strung along the fence. It is the Fourth of July.* JASPER, *in his early thirties, wearing shorts and a T-shirt, is trying to light the grill by pushing an ignition button, but it's not catching.* DAN, *also in his early thirties, is standing beside him, drinking a beer. He wears long madras shorts and an ironic T-shirt of some sort—such as the* Electric Company *logo or* Lemonheads *candy logo. He wears black Converse sneakers or flip-flops, and perhaps a baseball cap.*]

DAN: Is the gas on?

JASPER: Yes.

DAN: You're gonna have to get a match. Do you have a fireplace match?

JASPER: No.

DAN: Here—turn off the gas and we'll light a newspaper or something.

[JASPER *turns off the gas.*]

JASPER: I'll get it.

[JASPER *heads toward the door of the first-floor apartment.* MELINDA *and* WINDSONG *are coming out of it, carrying bowls, plates, and other dishes.* WINDSONG *is seven months pregnant. They are both fashionably, if casually, dressed.*]

MELINDA: Do you need something?

JASPER: A newspaper. I got it.

[JASPER *goes inside.*]

WINDSONG: She said she's going to make a diaper cake.

MELINDA: Oh yeah. She had one at her shower.

DAN: What the hell's a diaper cake?

MELINDA: You roll up diapers and stack them up on this little plastic tray, then you put little toys and ribbons on it, sort of swirled around so it looks like a cake.

WINDSONG: Are you supposed to eat it?

MELINDA: It's a centerpiece.

WINDSONG: Oh.

MELINDA: Everybody loved it.

[MELINDA *hands an aluminum foil–covered plate to* DAN.]

We should make the turkey burgers first. [*To* WINDSONG] It took you guys eight months, right?

WINDSONG: Seven, I guess. I didn't know until eight.

DAN: You're supposed to give yourself a year before you worry.

MELINDA: I just never thought so much about my stupid period before.

WINDSONG: It's only been a few months.

DAN: Don't worry. It's totally going to happen for you guys.

[JASPER *comes out with a sheet of newspaper, which he is rolling up tightly.*]

MELINDA: I just thought it would happen sooner.

DAN [*to* JASPER]: Our doctor said to give it a year before you worry. So I wouldn't worry.

JASPER [*looking to* MELINDA]: I think we're patient . . .

MELINDA: I told them I got my period.

JASPER: Right.

DAN: We don't have to talk about it.

JASPER: We can talk about it.

MELINDA: It took them seven months.

WINDSONG: And you have to try for two years before they'll even consider infertility treatments.

DAN: Next Fourth of July, we'll be swarming with kids. Let's fire this thing up.

[DAN *turns on the gas.* JASPER *lights the newspaper with a match.*]

MELINDA: What are you doing?

JASPER: It won't light.

MELINDA [*alarmed*]: What are you doing?

JASPER: It won't light.

DAN: Stick it up under there.

MELINDA: Jasper.

[MELINDA *and* WINDSONG *stand far back.* JASPER *sticks the lit news-paper into the grill, which lights. A sound effect of a muffled boom would be nice.*]

   [*Worried*] You're going to burn your eyebrows off.

JASPER [*to the others*]: Melinda's eighth-grade English teacher didn't have any eyebrows.

MELINDA: She drew them on every morning with a pencil.

[*Small beat. This is a bad memory.*]

   One morning she forgot.

DAN: You guys want some music?

JASPER: Yeah.

[JASPER *starts loading things on the grill.*]

MELINDA: That's kind of a lot, isn't it?

JASPER: It cooks better with more on.

MELINDA: How do you figure?

JASPER: All the flavor builds up and . . . flavorizes.

WINDSONG: What time do the fireworks start?

MELINDA: Nine, I think.

[DAN *pulls out a CD.*]

DAN: When d'you get this?

JASPER [*glancing at the CD*]: A while ago. It was used.

MELINDA: Don't put on anything too loud. Our landlords are coming.

WINDSONG: Did you ask them about the shower?

MELINDA: They said it was fine. They're going to be out of town anyway.

WINDSONG: They're so nice.

DAN: Who all's coming to this shower anyway?

WINDSONG: Everybody.

DAN: Boys and girls?

WINDSONG: Yes, boys and girls.

DAN: I hope we get good presents. Hey—did you see?—you can get your baby these onesies with, like, bands on them. Good bands. Like the Dead Kennedys.

MELINDA: Really?

JASPER: That depresses me for some reason.

WINDSONG: Or we saw one that said, I might vomit.

[WINDSONG *giggles.*]

DAN: Here we go.

[DAN *puts on a CD of Brazilian samba music.*]

JASPER: Always a crowd-pleaser.

DAN: It's your CD.

[DAN *takes* WINDSONG *by the hand and starts to dance with her.* MELINDA *sets the table.*]

JASPER: Tom and Karen just got back from Costa Rica. They rented a car and drove down the coast. They were telling me about it last night . . .

[*No one is listening to* JASPER.]

It sounded pretty cool.

WINDSONG: Ouch.

[DAN *and* WINDSONG *stop dancing.*]

DAN: Sciatica?

WINDSONG: Yeah.

[DAN *goes to the washtub and gets a beer.* WINDSONG *follows.*]

MELINDA [*to* JASPER]: Why does it depress you?

JASPER: What?

MELINDA: The Dead Kennedys onesie.

JASPER: Okay. You just said, "Dead Kennedys onesie." That doesn't . . .

MELINDA: What?

JASPER: It's supposed to be, like, rebellious-counter-culture-music-you-listen-to-when-you're-fifteen-to-drive-your-parents-crazy. Not, you know, an accessory. For your baby.

MELINDA: I think it's funny.

JASPER: It's just that I kind of feel like everything I ever liked is being appropriated by idiots and completely ruined.

[WINDSONG *is rummaging around in the washtub.*]

MELINDA: They wouldn't make it if it didn't sell.

WINDSONG [*to* DAN]: I thought you bought me some near beer.

DAN: I don't see how you can drink that crap.

WINDSONG: I feel all left out when everybody's drinking.

JASPER: You know, I'm pretty positive my mom drank like a fish when she was pregnant with me, so you must have to really—

DAN [*interrupting*]: Yeah, like it was fine until 1980, and then all of a sudden one beer and your baby's brain-dead.

MELINDA: It's called fetal alcohol syndrome.

JASPER: Then why don't I have it?

MELINDA [*smiling*]: Who says you don't?

[*The screen door upstairs opens and closes, then* TOM *and* KAREN *come downstairs, carrying a bag of fruit, a cutting board, a knife, and red wine in a pitcher. They are both casually dressed. You couldn't peg them for anything by their clothes.*]

TOM: Are we starting?

KAREN: Hi there.

MELINDA: Hey, guys.

[KAREN *and* TOM *start to come downstairs.*]

You remember Windsong and Dan, don't you?

TOM: Of course. How are you?

WINDSONG: Good.

DAN [*overlapping*]: Real good.

WINDSONG: Thanks so much for saying we could have our baby shower in your yard.

KAREN: Oh. No problem.

WINDSONG: We'd love for you guys to come.

TOM: We're going out of town. But thank you.

KAREN: We thought we'd make sangria. I just brought everything down. In case someone didn't like some particular sort of fruit.

TOM: Karen likes to use blueberries. Are blueberries okay?

MELINDA: That sounds great.

[KAREN *and* TOM *come out into the yard.*]

TOM [*shaking* DAN's *hand*]: So, you two, congratulations are in order.

DAN: Thanks.

KAREN [*to* WINDSONG]: You look very happy and healthy.

WINDSONG: I am. I really am.

KAREN: Good for you.

[*Pause.*]

MELINDA: You guys probably haven't seen each other since our Christmas party last year.

[KAREN *starts making sangria.* TOM *helps.*]

TOM: That's right.

DAN [*to* TOM]: You were working on somebody's campaign, right?

JASPER: Managing it.

TOM: Jennifer Baldwin. For the House.

DAN: She won, right?

TOM: Beat the incumbent.

WINDSONG: We campaigned for Kerry up in Milwaukee. It kind of sucks, living in a blue state, because there's not a lot you can do.

[*Beat.*]

It was just one day. We hung things on people's doorknobs.

KAREN: So when are you due?

WINDSONG: October.

KAREN: That's exciting. This is your first?

WINDSONG: Yes. [*To* MELINDA] Did I tell you, I asked about maternity leave and Mr. Wisneski told me I had six weeks, but he'd only pay me for two.

KAREN: Are you still at the museum?

WINDSONG: The Polish-American Museum.

KAREN: How many employees?

WINDSONG: Fifteen?

TOM: Tell us what you do there again, Windsong.

WINDSONG: Oh. Publications director. Which basically means I write and edit the newsletter. I'm going to quit.

KAREN: You don't like it?

WINDSONG: It sucks. Not to be anti-Polish, but they're a bunch of thugs. They hate Lech Walesa. You bring up Solidarity and they start laughing. They think he's a rube. [*To* KAREN] You work for a union, right?

KAREN: UFCW.

WINDSONG: That's very cool, I think. We worked out of the AFL-CIO headquarters. In Milwaukee. When we campaigned. There were tons of union people there.

TOM: Karen was there.

WINDSONG: You were?

TOM: For almost . . . ten weeks.

WINDSONG: Wow.

DAN: Did we even win Wisconsin?

KAREN AND TOM: Yes.

[*Beat.*]

KAREN: I forgot the sugar.

TOM: I'll get it.

[TOM *starts to head upstairs.*]

I can't wait for the fireworks. It's all nationalistic crap, I know. But I don't care.

KAREN: They're pretty. I like the ones with the little spirally things.

WINDSONG: Like curlicue things. I love those.

KAREN: So will you look for another job? After the baby's born?

WINDSONG [*looking at* DAN]: I don't know. I have a master's in English, you know. So I was thinking, maybe, after the baby's born, I could do some freelance editing from home.

DAN: With child care it kind of doesn't make any sense for her to work full-time. We wouldn't be ahead, in the end.

KAREN: Well, there's no point in doing something if you can't be ahead in the end.

JASPER: Does anybody want chicken? We marinated some chicken.

KAREN: Chicken sounds great.

[JASPER *opens a Tupperware container.*]

DAN: Where are you guys going?

KAREN: I'm sorry?

DAN: When we're having our shower. You said you were going out of town.

KAREN: Oh. Tom has a conference down in Springfield. There's a really good used-book store I like down there, so I thought I'd tag along.

MELINDA: Do you want to maybe take something off, before you put that on?

JASPER: It's going to get all smoky and . . . flavorize.

KAREN: Are you still working on that economics textbook, Jasper?

JASPER [*nodding*]: It's astounding.

KAREN: How's that?

[*The screen door slams again as* TOM *comes back down the stairs. During the following, he brings* KAREN *the sugar.*]

JASPER: Oh, little things. Like when they talk about Sweden, they say that even though the state provides every citizen with free health care and a free education and a pension and [*to* WINDSONG] a year's maternity leave, all of that comes at a "very high price," which, comparatively—

DAN [*interrupting*]: They should get free Saabs.

JASPER: They levy a twenty percent income—

DAN [*interrupting*]: Their suicide rate is huge, apparently. In the middle of the winter, everybody's like, "Ja, I can't take it anymore." And they go jump in the fjords.

[*Beat.*]

KAREN [*to* JASPER]: You were saying . . . ?

JASPER: Just—we tax at eleven or twelve percent—it doesn't seem like any sort of bargain to me, considering what you get for your money.

KAREN: We got an illegal war.

TOM: And chaos. We got chaos.

DAN: What time do you guys want to head to the lake?

MELINDA: I thought eight-thirty.

DAN: I want to get a good spot.

KAREN: So do I.

TOM: It's nationalistic crap but we love the explosions.

KAREN: You said that already.

TOM: I did?

WINDSONG: Doesn't it scare you?

TOM: Alzheimer's?

WINDSONG: The war, the Middle East. It all scares me.

JASPER: Windsong is scared of raccoons.

KAREN: Really?

JASPER: And mice and nighthawks and bats . . .

MELINDA: Jasper.

WINDSONG: I'm not a big outdoors person. Okay? [*To* KAREN] I just meant that, because I'm having the baby, I actually feel scared now, where before I would just get pissed off.

KAREN: Well of course you're scared. The world's probably going to end in your baby's lifetime.

TOM: Are you having a boy or a girl?

WINDSONG [*slightly stunned*]: A girl.

DAN [*to* WINDSONG]: The world is not going to end in Iris's lifetime. Iris is going to change the world.

KAREN: Well, it might not end, but it will definitely be . . . you know. Awful.

[*Beat.*]

MELINDA [*to* TOM *and* KAREN]: They're naming the baby Iris.

TOM: That's lovely. You don't hear names like that anymore.

WINDSONG: Do you think it's too trendy? To have an old-fashioned name?

DAN: It's your great-aunt's name. It's not like we just pulled it out of thin air.

KAREN [*to* MELINDA]: How's work for you, Melinda? Are you still working on that Michigan project?

MELINDA: It's endless. We just finished writing the field tests.

WINDSONG: Did you find out what kind of maternity leave you get?

MELINDA [*uncomfortably*]: No. Not yet.

KAREN: Are you pregnant?

MELINDA: No.

JASPER: No.

[*Beat.*]

We're trying.

KAREN: I didn't know you wanted children.

MELINDA: Yeah.

KAREN: Since when?

MELINDA: Um, I guess we started, like, five months ago?

WINDSONG: It took us a year. [*To* MELINDA] Maybe you should start taking your temperature. There's no point if you're not ovulating.

DAN [*laughing*]: We saw this improv group a while back. They had this routine where this couple was listing all the reasons they never had sex, you know, "The cat's on the bed" or "Tom Cruise is on Conan." And the tag was, "We're just not the fucking types."

WINDSONG [*laughing*]: I'm always like, "I want to finish this article in the *New Yorker*."

DAN: We had more sex trying to get pregnant than we'd had in years.

WINDSONG: Now we don't have to do it anymore.

DAN: Thank God.

[DAN *and* WINDSONG *laugh.*]

TOM: I guess if you feel like you're doing it for a reason, it might take some of the fun out of it.

DAN: Talk about performance anxiety.

MELINDA: Don't, okay?

[MELINDA *looks at* JASPER.]

JASPER: What? I'm not—

MELINDA: I know, but—

JASPER: He's not going to jinx me. God.

DAN: What's the matter, buddy? Little guy not snapping to attention?

JASPER: There's not a problem.

DAN: Good. [*To* TOM *and* KAREN] He's prone.

WINDSONG: Dan!

DAN: Not to that. To nervous tics and shit. That's why I'm always telling you not to worry. [*To* TOM *and* KAREN] When they got married, he couldn't move his head.

JASPER: I was sleeping on this fold-out—

DAN [*interrupting*]: He had this massive crick in his neck, and in all the pictures, he's staring straight ahead like he's robot-boy. "Danger, Will Robinson. Danger!"

[WINDSONG *and* MELINDA *laugh. Whatever the picture was of* JASPER, *it was very funny. They can't control themselves.*]

JASPER: Thanks a lot.

MELINDA: It was only one picture and we didn't order it.

DAN: You should have kept the proof.

MELINDA: No!

WINDSONG: It looked like his head was Photoshopped onto his body.

[WINDSONG, MELINDA, *and* DAN *laugh.*]

JASPER: I'm so glad you find this amusing.

MELINDA: I'm sorry.

[DAN *and* WINDSONG *are still giggling.*]

Guys, stop!

DAN: We'll stop.

WINDSONG: We promise.

[DAN *and* WINDSONG *stop. Beat.*]

TOM: So you want to be parents.

MELINDA: We sort of turned a corner last year.

TOM: Did something in particular happen?

MELINDA: It was just sort of abstract before that. But then that completely clichéd thing happened where I started seeing babies and wanting to grab them. And it seemed like I was telling myself something. That we were ready to move forward.

KAREN: Well. Then. The timing is probably good.

JASPER: Yeah?

KAREN: Well, your lease is up in October. So you could move before anything happens.

TOM: If you want to move to a bigger place.

KAREN: Which everyone does. Who wants sangria?

[KAREN *starts to pour.*]

WINDSONG: That looks great.

KAREN: So is this something your parents want you to do?

JASPER: My parents do. Not that I care. But they do. And Windsong's parents really used to pressure us—

WINDSONG: They did?

KAREN [*overlapping*]: Why?

JASPER: Because . . .

MELINDA: You said, "Windsong's parents."

JASPER: I did?

[JASPER *laughs.*]

That's weird.

DAN: Yeah.

[*Everyone looks at* JASPER.]

MELINDA: *My* parents used to pressure us. Then I think they gave up.

JASPER: And your sister had kids.

MELINDA: And Suzanne had kids. So they sort of focused on her.

KAREN: Sure.

MELINDA: That's not why we're doing it, though.

TOM: Then why are you?

MELINDA: Because.

DAN: You have to replace yourself in the gene pool.

KAREN: You do?

DAN: Yeah.

JASPER: Why?

DAN: Because you'll disappear otherwise.

JASPER: And?

DAN: You want to leave a mark, don't you? I mean, what else am I going to leave behind? [*To* TOM] I write for the *Tribune.* Music reviews.

TOM: I know.

DAN: Which, they're already obsolete by the time they come out. Because the concert's over. Or the CD's already in the bargain bin. It's pretty friggin' fleeting. So that's no legacy there. So if you don't have kids, then what do you leave behind?

KAREN [*to* MELINDA]: It's funny, because when you talk about your sister and her children, you never seem to enjoy them really . . .

MELINDA: Because they're awful. They watch TV twenty-four hours a day and they're always playing video games . . . Which—I look at that as a negative example. We're not going to do it like that.

WINDSONG: God no.

KAREN: Would you quit working?

MELINDA: No, I definitely want to keep working.

KAREN: Well that's good, at least.

[*Beat.*]

TOM [*more toward* KAREN *than* MELINDA]: It's great you want to have kids.

KAREN [*hearing* TOM *and to* MELINDA]: If that's what you want, then we hope it works out.

[*Pause.*]

JASPER: I think the burgers are ready. [*To* MELINDA] Should we wait for Dwight?

DAN: He won't care.

MELINDA: Is the chicken done?

JASPER: No, but whoever wants burgers can eat burgers.

MELINDA: I think some people wanted chicken.

JASPER: We don't all have to eat at the same time, do we?

MELINDA: It's kind of rude . . .

KAREN: We don't care.

TOM [*overlapping*]: We really don't care.

JASPER: How 'bout—I'll just put them on a plate and you can put the foil back over them, okay?

MELINDA: Okay.

WINDSONG [*to* DAN]: Can I have a sip of your sangria?

[DAN *hands* WINDSONG *the glass.*]

DAN: One sip. [*To* KAREN] Did you drink when you were pregnant? Because we feel like this is a recent thing.

KAREN: I've never been pregnant.

DAN: I thought you had kids.

KAREN: No.

DAN: Oh. I thought you had like a grown daughter, or something.

KAREN: No.

DAN: By choice?

KAREN: Yes.

DAN: Too busy being kids to have kids, huh?

WINDSONG: It's hard to have a career and kids . . .

KAREN: I am not a child.

DAN: I'm just kidding.

[Beat.]

KAREN [to WINDSONG]: I've always wanted to ask you about your name. Is it a nickname?

WINDSONG: My parents were stupid hippies. I think they were half-baked when they picked it out.

JASPER [teasing]: Isn't Windsong a perfume?

WINDSONG: Shut up.

JASPER [singing]: "I can't seem to forget you . . ."

WINDSONG: Stop it.

MELINDA: Windsong's parents live in Gary Hart's old town house. In Georgetown.

KAREN: We campaigned for Gary Hart.

TOM: 1984.

[*Beat.*]

DAN: I was eleven.

WINDSONG [*to* TOM *and* KAREN]: So you guys are really active.

TOM: We jog . . .

WINDSONG: I mean, politically active. You've always been that way.

TOM: Yeah.

WINDSONG: That's really cool, I think. My parents were when they were young, but then they sold out.

TOM: What do they do?

WINDSONG: My dad's an investment banker.

DAN: Her dad knows Alan Greenspan.

WINDSONG: Alan Greenspan used to play the clarinet, then he played one night with Stan Getz and he said, "I'll never be as good as that," and he quit.

KAREN: Who's as good as Stan Getz? How long had Stan Getz been playing? It's not even the same instrument. What he thought was, "I can't beat Stan Getz, so I'll quit."

[*Beat.*]

DAN: He was good for the economy.

WINDSONG: I miss Bill Clinton.

MELINDA: Did you see—there was a button over at the record store that said, "Would somebody please give George W. Bush a blow job so that we can impeach him?"

[*Everyone laughs.*]

The thing is, who's going to volunteer to do that?

DAN: Not Laura.

WINDSONG: Why is she married to him?

KAREN: Because she wants to be. [*To* DAN] The Clinton economy was great, for a certain group of people—people like you or me—but he basically dismantled the social safety net for everyone else. He was just a stalking horse for the Republicans.

TOM [*to* DAN]: This is Karen's job, you know. Fighting the government and these giant corporations, trying to get people a living wage—

WINDSONG: You should unionize Wal-Mart.

TOM: That's exactly what she's trying to do.

KAREN: I don't think we'd be where we are today if Clinton hadn't sold us out.

DAN: That's where Nader was totally right. There was no difference between the two parties.

KAREN: Ralph Nader's an idiot. Anybody who voted for Ralph Nader should be pistol-whipped.

[*Beat.*]

JASPER: Dan voted for Nader.

KAREN [*to* DAN]: Oh. I'm sorry.

[*Beat.*]

I shouldn't have said that about being pistol-whipped.

DAN [*recovering*]: Hey. Did you say "pistol-whip"? Because I thought you said "Miracle Whip." And Miracle Whip makes one helluva sammich.

[*General laughter. Beat.*]

MELINDA: Speaking of which—is that chicken ready?

JASPER: I'm cooking it on low . . .

MELINDA: I made this guacamole. Have some guacamole.

[MELINDA *passes around chips and gets the guacamole.*]

TOM [*taking some*]: Thank you, Melinda.

DAN: What are these red things in here?

MELINDA: Pomegranates.

DAN: Freaky.

WINDSONG: It's good. [*To* KAREN] Melinda's a good cook, I think.

KAREN: I know. I'm going to miss her cooking.

MELINDA: You know, I don't know that we were thinking of moving right away.

JASPER: We're nowhere near thinking about that.

KAREN: But the place is really too small for a family.

MELINDA: But I'm not even pregnant.

WINDSONG [*to* KAREN]: You won't have any trouble renting their place. If that's what you're worried about. It's a great place.

TOM: It's not that. It's just . . . sometimes it's easier to go ahead and move. Than trying to move when you have a baby.

KAREN: It's less of a hassle.

JASPER: We really . . . We thought we'd stay for the first year at least.

DAN: So do you guys not want kids in your building?

[*Beat.*]

TOM: Well, Karen and I made a very deliberate decision not to have children.

KAREN: It's not that we don't like children. We do.

TOM: It's sort of the same reason we don't allow pets. You have a dog, you go out for the night, it starts barking. You have a baby, it's three in the morning, it starts crying . . .

KAREN: We can't codify it, of course. That's illegal.

TOM: We just hope, since it's our home as well, that whoever is renting from us will respect our wishes.

MELINDA: Seriously?

JASPER [*overlapping*]: Wow.

KAREN: It's nothing personal.

TOM: Quite the contrary.

DAN: But you let our band practice in your basement. That's louder than a baby.

TOM: But you always stop at ten. Babies don't stop at ten.

DAN [*to* MELINDA *and* JASPER]: Don't stay where you're not wanted.

KAREN: It's not that you're not wanted. We've really enjoyed having you.

TOM: We really have.

KAREN: It's just that everyone who's had a baby has left. We've learned it's easier just to get it over with.

[*Beat.* MELINDA *and* JASPER *consider. Then . . .*]

MELINDA [*to* JASPER]: We were going to buy anyway . . .

JASPER: I guess . . .

WINDSONG: Come look with us.

DAN: Yeah, come look with us.

WINDSONG: I really want us all to be in the same neighborhood.

MELINDA: Us too.

[JASPER *doesn't say anything.*]

WINDSONG: We looked at some condos over near Rosehill that we really liked.

MELINDA: What school district is that?

WINDSONG: It doesn't matter. We're doing the magnet thing.

TOM: Who's the alderman there?

WINDSONG: Why?

TOM: I worked for O'Connelly this last year and people were coming to his door at night, begging for some sort of intervention.

WINDSONG [*alarmed*]: To get into the magnet schools?

TOM: But I'm sure . . . You're very resourceful people. If you can navigate bureaucracies, you're fine.

JASPER: What if . . . I could put up some sort of soundproofing board, like they use in recording studios.

TOM: There's also the clutter. First the stroller in the entryway, then all the stuff in the backyard.

KAREN: The half-deflated balls. The tricycle. The wading pool.

JASPER: We don't have to have all that.

WINDSONG [*to* DAN]: Maybe we should just buy a house in Evanston.

DAN: We're keeping our Chicago address.

WINDSONG: But now I'm panicking about schools.

DAN: It's a long way off.

WINDSONG [*to* TOM]: I heard people actually put their fetuses on the waiting list to get into the Montessori school.

DAN: Worse comes to worse, we can homeschool her.

WINDSONG: No we can't.

DAN: You can teach her how to read *Lucky*.

KAREN: What's that?

DAN: A magazine about *shopping*. She reads it religiously.

WINDSONG: I'm trying to talk to you about schools.

DAN: But there's nothing we can do about it right now, is there? So why talk about it?

[DAN *gets another beer. Beat.*]

TOM: The days are so long this time of year.

WINDSONG: I only look at *Lucky* at the gym.

DAN: I know.

WINDSONG: I read all the time. I have a master's in English. I just read *Bleak House* for the third time.

DAN: I know.

WINDSONG: The only thing you read all year was Bob Dylan's autobiography.

DAN: And?

WINDSONG: Bob Dylan's stupid.

DAN: You can't say Bob Dylan is stupid.

WINDSONG: Yes I can.

DAN: He's not stupid, he's a fucking force of nature.

[*Pause.*]

TOM: Jasper, Melinda, I feel like we've put a real damper on everything with this talk of moving—

KAREN: I do, too.

TOM: We're very fond of both of you.

KAREN: We are.

TOM: Why don't we just say, it's a bridge we'll cross when we come to it?

JASPER [*to* MELINDA]: That seems fair. To just see what happens.

MELINDA: Maybe it's good. Maybe it'll make us make a decision sooner.

[TOM *takes a breath.*]

TOM [*to* DAN]: So you're a Dylan fan?

DAN [*abruptly*]: Yeah. I've seen him, like, twenty times in concert.

TOM: I saw him . . . probably thirty years ago. With The Band.

DAN: With The Band, The Band?

TOM: Yes.

DAN: The 1974 *Before the Flood* tour?

TOM: Sounds right.

DAN: Oh my God. That is so fucking awesome! [*Excited*] He gives of himself entirely, doesn't he? Every time. I totally admire him. I always have. I remember, I worked at this record store in Ann Arbor, when I was in college, and I remember, the guy that owned it had on a CD he'd made, and "Positively 4th Street" came up, and I was standing there . . . It's an obvious song to love, but I love it. And I was listening to it and he looked at me, and, I don't know, there was something in my face, or something, but he said, "You really get this, don't you?" And I just nodded because I didn't want to ruin it. It was . . . There's certain things you feel a connection to, on a visceral level . . . I don't even know how to say it. That whole sense of betrayal that song conveys. At the time, I felt, like, there aren't a whole lot of people on my side.

MELINDA: Why'd you feel that?

DAN: My family. My dad. He thought, if I was going to be a journalist, then I should be Woodward and Bernstein. He thinks music journalism is tripe, basically. Corporate shilling. I keep telling him how I promote these independent bands, you know, that self-produce, but then I try to get him to listen to something and he says, "All I hear is noise." It's maddening.

WINDSONG: Dan told his dad to go fuck himself.

MELINDA: You did?

WINDSONG: When they were in town last weekend.

DAN: It really upset him.

KAREN: Why would that upset him?

MELINDA: What did he do?

WINDSONG: We went out to dinner and he was being so pissy about the baby, and he kept saying, "You know, you're not going to have the freedom you have now. You're not going to get to listen to live music anymore . . ."

MELINDA: He's totally jealous of you.

WINDSONG: That's what Dan said. He said, "What? Are you afraid I'm going to ruin my life like you did yours?" [*To* KAREN *and* TOM] His dad always wanted to be a sportswriter.

KAREN: What stopped him?

DAN: Kids. I mean, my mom got pregnant and he had to marry her. So not kids, but . . . you know.

KAREN: Kids.

DAN: Right. So my dad said, "Well I guess I'm not a big shot, like you are—" Some people in the restaurant had recognized me, by my picture in the paper—he was like, "Just because I don't have a big byline in some newspaper. Just because I'm not the big man." And I just looked at him, and I said, "You know what, Dad? Go fuck yourself."

WINDSONG: Right in the middle of the restaurant. Everybody was staring at us.

DAN: Whatever. He doesn't get to talk to me like I'm twelve anymore.

KAREN: Maybe he got confused because you still dress like you're twelve.

[*Everyone looks at* KAREN.]

I'm kidding. Aren't we all kidding? Isn't that the vernacular here?

[KAREN *sighs.*]

I'm sorry, Dan. Please . . . don't let me interrupt.

DAN: No. I'm finished.

[*Beat.*]

JASPER [*singing in a very whiny imitation of Bob Dylan*]: "You have a lot of nerve, to say you are my friend . . ." Couldn't the guy at least throw in a chorus? Verse, verse, verse, verse. Thirty seconds of that and you're lulled into a vegetative state.

DAN: I don't know what to tell you.

JASPER [*singing again*]: "Tangled up in *blue.*"

[*He goes very high on* blue. KAREN *giggles and hides it.*]

WINDSONG [*to* KAREN]: There are going to be kids at our shower, is that okay?

KAREN: Yes.

WINDSONG: But isn't that why you're not coming?

TOM: We have to help one of Karen's coworkers move to Batavia.

DAN: What?

KAREN [*to* TOM]: You're going to a conference in Springfield.

TOM: Oh. Right.

[*Small beat.*]

Oops.

MELINDA [*to* JASPER]: Couldn't you just turn up the heat?

[JASPER *opens the grill and takes a piece of chicken with his tongs.*]

JASPER: It's already pretty stiff.

DAN: You need to get a meat thermometer.

JASPER: I can tell when it's done.

DAN: You grill the hell out of everything. It comes out like jerky.

JASPER: You don't have to eat it.

MELINDA [*forcefully*]: We need cutlery. Does anybody want something different to drink? Water? We have Coke.

JASPER: I need a beer.

MELINDA: Have a beer, then. I'll get forks.

[MELINDA *exits into their apartment.* JASPER *gets a beer.*]

JASPER: Who needs another beer?

DAN: I do.

KAREN [*overlapping*]: I'll take one.

TOM: Me too.

[JASPER *hands out beers.* DAN *picks up an empty sangria glass and looks at* WINDSONG.]

DAN: Did you drink all that sangria?

WINDSONG: There was hardly any left.

DAN: The doctor said a sip was okay . . .

WINDSONG: That's all I had.

DAN: That was a whole glass.

WINDSONG: I had one sip!

[*The gate in the fence opens, and* DWIGHT *enters, carrying a black, plastic, liquor-store bag with a six-pack in it.*]

DWIGHT: Hey. Sorry I'm late.

WINDSONG: Great. Dwight's here.

DWIGHT: You're pregnant.

WINDSONG: People keep saying that, like it's news or something.

DWIGHT: Your breasts are huge.

DAN: Dude.

DWIGHT [*seeing* KAREN *and* TOM]: Hey.

TOM: Hello.

[*Beat.*]

I'm Tom. I don't think we've formally met.

KAREN: We've seen you around. I'm Karen.

DWIGHT: Hey.

JASPER: And this is Dwight.

DWIGHT: Yeah. Right.

JASPER: Help yourself to a beer, Dwight.

DWIGHT: What do you have?

DAN: What did you bring?

JASPER: I think there's some Pilsner Urquell in there.

DWIGHT: Give me one of those.

[DWIGHT *gets a beer, takes his six-pack out of the bag, and puts it in the washtub.* DAN *watches.*]

DAN: MGD in cans?

DWIGHT: What?

DAN: There should be some rule that says you have to drink the beer you bring.

DWIGHT: What?

DAN: You always bring shit that nobody wants, then you drink the expensive beer and leave your fucking, *Icehouse,* to sit in my fridge for a year until I finally throw it away.

DWIGHT: You should never throw away beer.

[DWIGHT *takes a chip.*]

[*To* KAREN *and* TOM] Do you guys work with Melinda or something?

KAREN: We live upstairs.

DWIGHT: You're the landlords.

TOM: That's right.

DWIGHT: That's totally cool of you to let us use your basement.

JASPER: We need to rehearse this week.

DWIGHT: I can't, man. I'm swamped.

DAN: With what?

DWIGHT: Business.

[*Beat.*]

KAREN: Have you written any new songs lately?

DAN: Why? Do you think we need new songs?

KAREN: I wasn't saying that.

TOM: We're not always here when you rehearse.

KAREN: But every time we hear you, you play the same ten songs.

[*Beat.*]

DAN: Music is really important to me.

KAREN: Okay.

DAN: That's one thing I'm going to insist on with the baby. That she learn to play an instrument. In fact, we're thinking about sending her to the performing arts high school so she can train to be a musician.

WINDSONG: My parents said they'd pay for Montessori, if we couldn't get her in anywhere—

DAN: We're getting her into a magnet school. She's going to be musical and creative, but more important, she's going to be a truly interesting person.

[KAREN *knows this is directed at her.*]

She's going to be beautiful and generous and kind, like her mother, and she's going to be smart and funny and spiritual. Our daughter is going to make the world a better place—

KAREN: How is she going to do that, exactly?

DAN [*overlapping*]: And she's going to do that by building people up, not tearing them down.

[MELINDA *enters during this, carrying silverware wrapped in napkins. She stops on the porch.* KAREN *doesn't see her.*]

KAREN: That might make her a great sorority sister, but it's hardly going to qualify her to save the world.

DAN: I think you do hate kids.

KAREN: Of course we don't.

DAN: But you don't want them anywhere near you.

KAREN: Because we never wanted children. Which means we don't want to live around children.

TOM: This is our home.

WINDSONG: But why don't you want children?

TOM: We just didn't.

DAN: Because you're selfish.

KAREN: No.

DAN: And angry.

TOM: I am not selfish and I am not angry.

WINDSONG: I just—it doesn't seem natural to not want children.

KAREN: You just said it. You have kids and you devote your life to them and then one day they turn to you in a restaurant and say, "Go fuck yourself."

MELINDA: But Dan's father never wanted to have children.

WINDSONG: Our baby's going to be the most important thing in the world to us.

KAREN: Then you have nothing to worry about.

DAN: We're not worried.

KAREN: Good.

[Beat.]

DWIGHT: Here's what I don't like about people with kids—

DAN: What the fuck?

DWIGHT: Since we've opened up the subject. [*To* KAREN *and* TOM] I'm a waiter, right? The people with the kids come in, and it's one of two things. Either they bring a whole refrigerator's worth of food with them, in these little Tupperware containers, or they don't bring anything. Both suck equally. If they bring in the food, it's like, they hand you a Tupperware full of some sort of mush and they ask you to take it back to the kitchen and put it in the microwave for thirty-six seconds, like you have nothing else to do and like there's a fucking microwave in the kitchen, which there isn't. So you take it back and you throw it under a warming lamp, for like two minutes, then you bring it back and they stick their finger in the mush and they ask you, "Could you warm it up for eleven more seconds?" And while they wait, they open Tupperware number two, which *always* has Cheerios in it. Always, always. Fucking *Cheerios*. Which the kids—they don't eat the Cheerios. They *throw* the Cheerios. They spread the Cheerios like seed, like they're seeding the restaurant with little Cheerio trees. These people leave their tables, and it's like a goddamn cereal . . . PB and J . . . booger . . . *tsunami* hit.

[DWIGHT *breathes.*]

But if they don't bring the food, it's fucking torture the other way. "Could the kitchen make, like, a bowl of plain pasta, with no sauce of any kind on it?" "Could he get a cheese pizza? But could you scrape the cheese off before you bring it out?" "Do you have, like, any kind of melon or fresh fruit in the kitchen? Could you just bring us a little bowl of cut-up fruit? Oh. That's a lot of fruit. Is that the only size bowl you have?" "Was this—did you make a cheese pizza? Because you have to make a cheese pizza and scrape off the cheese. If you didn't put the cheese on at first, then it's just a sauce pizza, and he won't eat it. He won't eat that."

[*Beat.*]

Eat this, asshole.

[DWIGHT *grabs his crotch.*]

WINDSONG: God.

DWIGHT: Here's an idea: Next time, go to Applebee's. There's a menu there, for kids. It's called a "kids' menu." Chicken fingers. Wieners in sauce. It's on the fucking menu. Along with a word search and a crazy maze. Here are your crayons. Go wild.

WINDSONG: Maybe the parents want to eat a decent meal. Did you ever think of that?

DWIGHT: Did you ever hear the word *babysitter?*

DAN [*to* KAREN *and* TOM]: So that's why you don't have children? Because maybe, some day, they get angry with you? So to avoid one unpleasant dinner you deny yourself a family?

KAREN: That's only one of about five hundred reasons.

DAN: That seems really cowardly to me.

TOM: We never wanted children. Is the real reason.

WINDSONG: Why not?

KAREN: See, that's like asking someone, "Why don't you buy a sod farm?" It's either something you really want to do or it's not.

DAN: A sod farm?

KAREN: Or show chickens. Why don't you raise show chickens?

DAN: What the fuck's a show chicken?

KAREN: Chickens. You breed for show. With fancy feathers.

TOM: Not to eat, but for breed competition . . .

MELINDA: That's not the same at all.

KAREN: In its appeal. It either strikes you or it doesn't.

MELINDA: Children are sort of universally striking, though.

WINDSONG: Show chickens aren't.

JASPER: But even if you don't want the baby, once the baby's born, people always say, you're suddenly hit with this overwhelming sense of love and responsibility. You've made this baby, and it hits you. Right then. That you've done this amazing thing. Even if before, you weren't sure how you felt about it. Right?

MELINDA [to JASPER]: Or before that even. From the minute you're pregnant you know you're in this remarkable thing together. You don't have to wait till the baby's born.

TOM: I guess, to say that you should have a baby, to find out if you want a baby, seems pretty absurd. To me.

KAREN: Because if you find out you were right in the first place, and you didn't want one . . .

TOM: Why would you want to stave off *potential* regret by doing something that you feel almost positive will cause you *great* regret?

MELINDA: Why are you so sure you'd regret it?

TOM: Because we don't want to do it.

MELINDA: Aren't you afraid of being lonely?

KAREN: Sure. We're lonely now sometimes.

TOM: Holidays are hard. Sometimes we feel like a charity case. Or . . . what was that thing from Rudolph?

KAREN: The Island of Misfit Toys.

TOM: Like that. So we usually just run and hide.

KAREN: We go to Hawaii for Christmas.

MELINDA: But . . .

KAREN: What happens when one of us dies?

MELINDA: Not to be morbid.

KAREN: I'd probably kill myself.

TOM: I might try and hang on. Out of principle.

[Beat.]

> My grandmother was in a home for years. And my mother would take me to see her, fairly often. And every time I'd look around and there were all these old people, sitting in the common room, staring at the TV. All alone. Even on Sundays, which you think would be the big day. And you have to figure, the majority of them had children. So where were their children? Why didn't they come?

KAREN: There's never a guarantee.

TOM: Is there more pain in having no one to come see you? Or in knowing there's someone out there who won't make the trip?

WINDSONG: God.

DWIGHT: Buzz stomp.

TOM: We're sixty. It's not like we haven't thought it through. And it's not like we're bad people. Just because we don't want to procreate.

[Beat.]

KAREN: But you kids should, if you want to.

TOM: Absolutely.

KAREN: Don't let anything we say stop you. [*To* TOM] You know, I have a little—

[KAREN *touches her head.*]

TOM [*overlapping*]: My knee has been hurting me all day.

KAREN: It has?

TOM: That old trick knee.

KAREN: We should get you upstairs then and get you some Advil.

TOM: That'd probably be best.

DAN: Your knee hurts?

KAREN: Thanks so much for having us.

JASPER: You're leaving?

KAREN: We'll get the pitcher from you later.

JASPER: But what about the fireworks?

KAREN: We've seen them a million times. [*Going up the stairs*] If we don't see you before the shower, have a great time.

TOM: Yes. Best of luck.

JASPER [*baffled*]: Okay. Guys. Good night.

KAREN [*disappearing*]: Good night.

TOM: Good night.

[TOM *and* KAREN *go out of sight. Beat. They start laughing at something.*]

[*Offstage*] Shhh.

KAREN: Sorry.

[TOM *and* KAREN *are still laughing. The audience hears the sound of their screen door closing, and then the inside door closing. Pause.*]

DAN: What the fuck was that?

JASPER: I have no idea.

MELINDA: That was so weird.

WINDSONG: What were they laughing at?

DAN: Why'd you even invite them?

MELINDA: It's their backyard.

WINDSONG: Were they laughing at us?

DWIGHT: Hanging out with old people is weird. When they don't act that much different than you. You think by that point they should be all wise or something.

JASPER: They are kind of wise.

MELINDA: How?

JASPER: They . . .

[JASPER *sighs.*]

They read.

DAN: What does that mean?

JASPER: They're very well informed and I enjoy my conversations with them, usually, and I'm sorry if we had some sort of falling-out. Is all.

MELINDA: That wasn't a falling-out. That was an eviction. It was a total rejection.

JASPER: I had no idea they felt so strongly about the kid thing . . .

WINDSONG: They're overcompensating. They know they made a mistake.

DAN: She's really offensive.

JASPER: They do have strong opinions. Which I, actually, have always found—

DAN [*interrupting*]: Judgmental?

JASPER [*louder*]: —Refreshing, because so often people approach their lives with this sort of ironic, dismissive—

DAN: Happiness?

JASPER [*louder still*]: —Tone, that keeps everything at a safe distance when—

DAN: Life is short, though. You gotta ease up.

[*Beat.* JASPER *stares at* DAN.]

JASPER: I guess one thing about Karen and Tom is that they are able to carry on an adult conversation. One crazy thing they do—which is practically unheard of—is they ask you questions about yourself. Can you imagine? Like, "How is work?" "What have you been doing lately?" "I would love to hear about your trip to Costa Rica." Not just questions, but open-ended questions, that allow you to respond at some length—

DAN: Are you talking about—

JASPER [*overriding him*]: Which you're able to do because they DO NOT INTERRUPT YOU!

[*Pause.*]

DAN: Are you directing that at me?

JASPER: You never let me talk.

WINDSONG: This is really bad.

DAN: Maybe because you analyze everything *to death*.

JASPER: Because I'm a curious person.

DAN: I read books, you know. I have a lot of books.

JASPER: You thought George Eliot was a man.

DAN: What?

MELINDA [*overlapping*]: Jasper . . .

JASPER: We were in a bookstore once, I was looking at *Middlemarch*, I said something about George Eliot, and you said, "Who's he?"

DAN: Because I don't know who the fuck he is!

JASPER: See?!

MELINDA: Guys!

DAN: It doesn't mean I'm stupid; it means I have a fucking life! I have better things to do besides sit on my ass reading every book ever published.

JASPER: Like what? Agonizing over whether the Arctic Monkeys should be number five or number six on your year-end top-ten list?

DWIGHT: I still can't believe you put fucking OK Go on your top-ten list.

DAN: They write solid pop licks and that is no easy task! Okay?! Asshole.

DWIGHT: Bite me.

MELINDA: Please!

WINDSONG [*overlapping*]: This is bad. This is so bad. Don't fight—
don't fight. You guys are our family! You're going to be Iris's aunt
and uncle. Don't let them make us fight! [*To* MELINDA, *pointing
upstairs*] They're ruining our lives.

JASPER: They're just our landlords—

WINDSONG: They're troublemakers!

[WINDSONG *puts her face in her hands.*]

 I don't feel good.

DAN: Honey?

WINDSONG: I don't. I don't feel good.

[WINDSONG *starts to cry.*]

 It's so hot.

DAN: Why'd you drink that sangria? You should be drinking water.

[DAN *looks around, helpless.* MELINDA *grabs a bottled water from the
washtub and takes it over to* WINDSONG.]

WINDSONG: I don't know if I want to name the baby Iris, Dan.

DAN: Nothing's engraved in stone.

WINDSONG: What if it's just a reaction formation to my stupid name?

MELINDA: Drink some water.

WINDSONG: God, you guys! Dan's parents are assholes and my parents
are fucking flakes! Our baby's going to be so fucking fucked up.

MELINDA: She is not.

WINDSONG: She's right! Everybody hates their parents. I don't know anybody who doesn't hate their parents.

DWIGHT: My parents are pretty cool, actually.

WINDSONG: See? If you don't hate them then you never separate from them and then you never grow up!

[WINDSONG *wipes her nose.*]

I'm getting snot everywhere.

JASPER [*handing* WINDSONG *a napkin*]: Here.

DAN: This is the hormones.

WINDSONG: It's not the fucking hormones! I can't get upset about anything without you saying it's hormones! You have such an aversion to anything complicated. Jasper's right. You never let anybody talk about anything!

[*Pause.*]

DAN [*quietly*]: I want people to be happy.

WINDSONG: Oh God, Dan. I'm sorry—

DAN: Some things you talk about forever and they never change.

WINDSONG: I know. I know.

[*Beat.*]

But sweetie, if she's got a problem, you're going to have to listen to her.

DAN [*upset*]: Of course I will.

WINDSONG: I know. Sweetie, I know.

[WINDSONG *blows her nose.* DAN *pulls her hair up off her neck and blows on her neck.* MELINDA *puts an ice cube in a napkin and hands it to* DAN.]

DAN: You got too hot.

MELINDA: Use this.

[DAN *rubs the napkin on her neck.*]

Everything's going to be okay.

[MELINDA *glares at* JASPER.]

JASPER: Yeah. It's going to be fine.

[MELINDA *continues to glare at* JASPER.]

Listen, buddy, I'm sorry I said all that. I just—I was being a prick. I'm sorry.

DAN: It's okay.

JASPER: I am. I'm a fucking blowhard.

DAN: Look, we have these things sometimes, and then it's said, and, you know, we get over it. You know me, I know you, so . . . You know. It's okay. We're over it.

[JASPER *nods vaguely.*]

So this barbecue is kind of a bust—

MELINDA: Guys, I don't know what happened . . .

JASPER: You know what? Let's put everything in a Tupperware, and either, we can all go watch the fireworks—

DAN: It's too hot.

JASPER: Then let's go get a beer—

MELINDA: Windsong can't—

WINDSONG [*overlapping*]: I can't sit in a smoky bar—

JASPER: Right. Sorry.

WINDSONG: I don't feel good.

DAN: You really don't?

WINDSONG: I really don't.

DAN: You want to go home?

WINDSONG: Yes.

DAN: Let's go home, then.

MELINDA: I feel so bad.

WINDSONG: You guys are still our friends, right?

MELINDA: Of course we are!

[MELINDA *and* WINDSONG *hug.*]

We love you guys so much.

DAN: We do too. You know? [*Holding out his hand out to* JASPER] Good night, man.

JASPER: I'm really sorry—

DAN: It's seriously okay. If we didn't fight, we wouldn't be family. So. Don't even think about it.

JASPER: Okay.

DAN: Okay.

MELINDA [*to* WINDSONG]: Call me tomorrow?

WINDSONG: I will.

MELINDA: Promise?

WINDSONG: Promise.

[WINDSONG *looks up at the second floor.*]

    I can't wait until you move.

DAN: Yeah. Bad vibes all around.

[DAN *and* WINDSONG *exit.*]

DWIGHT: So we're not going to eat?

JASPER: You can eat, if you want.

DWIGHT: I'm not really hungry.

[DWIGHT *pulls a dime bag out of his pocket.*]

    You guys want to get stoned?

JASPER: Not really.

DWIGHT: Homegrown, man. Good crop.

JASPER: No thanks.

DWIGHT: You want to buy some for later?

MELINDA: No.

DWIGHT: I might go, then.

[*Small beat.*]

JASPER: You want your beer back?

DWIGHT: Do you mind?

JASPER: Take it.

[DWIGHT *gets his six-pack.*]

DWIGHT: If you guys are going to move out of here, let me know, because this is a great apartment.

JASPER: Good night, Dwight.

DWIGHT: See ya.

[DWIGHT *exits.* JASPER *looks around.*]

JASPER: I'll clean all this up. Go to bed if you want.

MELINDA: It's, like, eight o'clock.

JASPER: Right.

[JASPER *starts cleaning up.* MELINDA *watches him. He looks at her and then forces a laugh.*]

Some Fourth of July, huh?

MELINDA: What is wrong with you?

JASPER: Because I yelled at Dan?

MELINDA: Because what is wrong with you.

JASPER: The guy gets on my nerves sometimes.

MELINDA: Maybe he has a different kind of intelligence than knowing who George Eliot is.

JASPER: Meaning?

MELINDA: He's your best friend.

JASPER: No, Dan is married to your best friend.

MELINDA: And he's your best friend.

[*Beat.*]

JASPER: Well that's depressing because the guy is really bad for my mental health.

MELINDA: You expect too much from him.

JASPER: I don't want to live an unexamined life.

MELINDA: Neither do I.

JASPER: I want to lead a meaningful life.

MELINDA: Do you not think we do?

JASPER: I just—I don't want to have a baby because they are.

MELINDA: What makes you say that?

JASPER: Just, like, a lot of times you and Windsong buy the same purse and stuff.

MELINDA: That's the stupidest thing I ever heard.

JASPER: You do everything together.

MELINDA: If it's happening at the same time, it's only because we're both thirty-five.

JASPER: Thirty-four.

MELINDA: I'm turning thirty-five in November.

JASPER: I know. I'm sorry.

[*Beat.*]

Maybe the thing with Dan is just—you know—do I look like him? Like, one of those guys?

MELINDA: What guys?

JASPER: The hipster dads. In the Converse sneakers and the baseball caps and the doofy, untucked shirts. Pushing their kids in the strollers, trying to act all engaged. "Look, Tyler. See the doggie? See the doggie with the bum? Hey, Tyler! Did you notice? Daddy's losing all sense of self!"

[MELINDA *regards him.*]

MELINDA: Who's Tyler?

JASPER: He's a fictional kid—

MELINDA: In a hypothetical world, but we're talking about real things.

JASPER: And that's just it—I keep seeing real things that completely freak me out. Like little things keep jumping out at me like they're on a spring or something. Like the other day, I was walking down Wilson and I walked by one house, and on the post, at the end of the banister, on the porch steps? There was this little toy giraffe sitting there. It was, maybe, four inches tall. Then the very next house, there was a jump rope wrapped around the banister and the handles were painted to look like ladybugs with a little face and wings?

[*He looks at* MELINDA *to see if she is following him. Small beat.*]

And then I noticed both houses had the same sort of ornamental shrubs, like, little evergreen trees that are trained to sort of droop over in a certain way? You'd think they were dying if you didn't know they were really expensive.

MELINDA: And?

JASPER: And everyone had the same thing in their yards, and if you have the kids, does that mean you have to buy the shrubs, too?

[MELINDA *doesn't answer.*]

You're not following me, are you?

MELINDA: I think I am.

JASPER: And?

MELINDA: We don't have to buy the shrubs. We don't have to do anything the way anybody else does it. We can do it however we want. [*Picking up a plate of food*] Do you care if I put all of this in one container?

JASPER: Am I not allowed to have doubts?

MELINDA: No, but . . .

JASPER: What?

[MELINDA *doesn't answer.*]

What?

MELINDA: Do you think this is why . . . ?

JASPER: What?

MELINDA: The other night . . . ?

JASPER: It was one time.

MELINDA: But maybe this is why.

JASPER: It was one time.

MELINDA: But I'm afraid it's because you're not sure.

JASPER: That's what I've been trying to say.

MELINDA: But we decided.

JASPER: No. You said you wanted to go off the pill and see what happened. And I said if you go off the pill, you'll probably get pregnant. Which is what you want, right?

MELINDA: But I want it to be what you want. Not something you go along with.

JASPER: But if I don't want it, what would you do? Go back on the pill?

MELINDA [*alarmed*]: You don't want children ever?

JASPER: I didn't say that.

MELINDA: Then what are you saying?

JASPER: I'm only trying to tell you I'm scared. That's all. I'm scared.

[*Beat.*]

MELINDA: I'm scared, too.

JASPER: See? Thank you. Right there. That makes me feel better, just to know. Because you seem so sure.

MELINDA: I seem so sure because you seem unsure. I feel like I have to be the rock.

JASPER: I don't want you to be a rock.

[*Small beat.*]

What are you afraid of?

MELINDA: I don't know. I mean, for a while I was afraid that it would mess up our lives, but lately I've been feeling like I kind of know what our life is now and I wouldn't mind if it was messed up.

JASPER: Thanks.

MELINDA: Don't you think we need a change?

JASPER: Couldn't we just paint the bathroom?

MELINDA [*regarding him*]: This is the other thing I'm afraid of. That you'll be a jerk.

[*Small beat.*]

I really appreciate that you're so smart and that you like to analyze things. But this isn't something you compile evidence for—

JASPER: It's a huge decision.

MELINDA: I know that. But sometimes it feels like we analyze things to death and we don't act. But we can't analyze this forever because there actually is a clock and if we wait too long we won't be able to have our own child. And that's what I want. Because I look at you and there are so many things I love about you, and our baby would have all those things. I think a kid that had all your best traits and whatever good traits I might have would be a really great kid. And maybe all our good traits would cancel out all the bad ones. I don't know, but think how much fun we'd have finding out. Because kids are, like, something new. Every day. Every day they discover some new thing, and it's probably something you've completely come to take for granted, but then they see it for the first time and it's brand new and it's *so cool.*

[*Beat.*]

And then all the crazy things they come up with. Like when we took Skip to the beach and he wouldn't stop talking about motors? "What would happen if you put a Lamborghini motor on a Jet Ski? What would happen if you put an outboard motor on a pickup truck?"

JASPER: "What if you took a lawn mower and welded it to a canoe?"

MELINDA: And I kept looking at him, thinking he's so much like your brother and Julie, and what a kick is that? To have more of the people you love in the world.

[*Beat.*]

JASPER: I'd love to have another one of you.

MELINDA: And I'd love to have another one of you.

[*Beat.*]

But then what if I never get pregnant?

JASPER: It's only been five months.

MELINDA: Everybody keeps saying that, but what's the problem? I'm young. I'm healthy.

JASPER: Which is all good, right?

[*Beat.*]

MELINDA: I thought I was pregnant this morning, when I woke up.

JASPER: You did?

MELINDA: It was total wishful thinking. But I felt funny and my boobs were all sore and I was really happy. Then I got my period.

JASPER: Why didn't you say something?

MELINDA: I wanted to surprise you at the fireworks. I thought it would be romantic.

JASPER: It's going to happen. We just have to be patient, okay?

[MELINDA *nods.*]

> Nobody's ever said they wanted another one of me in the world. That's like the nicest thing anyone's ever said to me.

[JASPER *puts his arm around* MELINDA. *They sit.*]

> Do you have cramps?

MELINDA: Yeah.

JASPER: Why don't you go inside and put on your pajamas and get the heating pad out?

MELINDA: No . . .

JASPER: I'll clean up out here and then we'll see if there's a good movie on. Okay?

MELINDA: It's not like I can't walk—

JASPER: It's okay.

[JASPER *kisses* MELINDA.]

> Go lie down.

MELINDA: You sure?

JASPER: Yeah. Go on. Or a baseball game. Or the election returns from Wisconsin.

[MELINDA *smiles.*]

MELINDA [*conceding*]: Okay. That was stupid. [*Starting to leave*] Everything's going to be fine.

JASPER: I know.

[MELINDA *goes in and closes the door behind her.* JASPER *stands for a moment, and then he starts putting up the folding chairs. He works. Then the sound of the door upstairs opening, then the screen door.* KAREN *and* TOM *come down the stairs.*]

KAREN: Jasper?

JASPER: Hello.

TOM: Hi.

KAREN: Hi.

[*Beat.*]

Where's Melinda?

JASPER: Inside. What's up?

KAREN: We wanted to apologize.

TOM: We tried to excuse ourselves before we drove your friends off entirely.

KAREN: Sometimes we forget that we're unfit for polite company. We're freaks.

JASPER: No—

KAREN: Statistically speaking. We're deliberately childless atheists.

TOM: I'm color-blind.

KAREN: The percentages get smaller and smaller.

[JASPER *laughs.*]

JASPER: It's all right, really. It was sort of a bad barbecue anyway.

TOM: Let us help you clean up at least.

JASPER: No, guys. Go see the fireworks.

TOM: There's still time.

KAREN: At least let us get all this fruit.

[KAREN *begins cleaning up the sangria ingredients.* TOM *helps.*]

JASPER: Thanks.

KAREN: So how do you know those guys?

JASPER: Dan and Windsong? They were Melinda's friends. From college.

TOM: Dan seems funny.

JASPER: He's very popular.

KAREN: And Windsong seems sweet.

JASPER: She thinks you guys are troublemakers.

[TOM *and* KAREN *smile.*]

We travel really well together. We enjoy traveling with them.

KAREN: That's nice.

[JASPER *works.*]

JASPER: Of course, I have two- or three-week periods where I'm like, "I can't possibly see them or I'm going to kill them." But then I take a break and it passes.

TOM: Uh-huh.

JASPER: It passes except for these fantasies I have in which I'm holding Dan's head down on the pavement and whacking his skull, over and over, with, like, a sledgehammer or a baseball bat. Or sort of putting my hand on Windsong's face and—not violently but with a steady amount of pressure—pushing her into a giant mud hole. I don't think I feel as strongly about killing Windsong because she's fairly dismissible. Except for the insane amount of influence she seems to have over my wife.

[JASPER *holds up a plastic container of cookies and looks at it.*]

You guys want these macaroons?

KAREN: We'd better not.

JASPER: The thing is, I've known her for twelve years and I still find her completely inscrutable. I have no idea what's going on in her head.

KAREN: Melinda?

JASPER: Windsong.

KAREN: Oh.

[KAREN *puts the knife in the pitcher. The sangria stuff is packed.* JASPER *stops what he's doing and sees that they've finished.*]

JASPER: If you'd had kids, how would you have wanted them to end up?

TOM: Boy. That's a new one.

KAREN: Not like your friends. No offense.

TOM: No.

KAREN: I guess . . . I love my nieces very much. I'd be proud to be their mother.

JASPER [*to* TOM]: And you have nephews, right?

TOM: They're twins. One's at Georgetown. One's at Brown. They're good kids.

KAREN: When they were little, they watched those programs on the TV with the loud, screaming voices. Do children really respond to that? Are there studies?

JASPER: My niece and nephew watch that crap, too. I guess they like it.

[Beat.]

My brother and I are both really into fly-fishing—my dad, too—we all tie our own flies? It's a family thing I really love—like, I'd love, if had a son, to teach him to fly-fish. That's one image I can really respond to.

KAREN: That's lovely.

JASPER: Oh yeah, if I could be anything, I'd be a fly-fishing guide.

KAREN: Why don't you?

[JASPER stares at KAREN. Pause.]

Was that not a good question?

JASPER: No—that's—my brother, see, he has two kids in a big—it's a big enough house, I think. And in the basement he has this little table set up, where he can tie flies. He goes down there on Friday nights—that's the big night—when he gets to tie flies and my sister-in-law works on her scrapbooks. And then maybe they read or watch TV until late—say, midnight even. That's their time because weeknights, otherwise, are consumed with homework and T-ball or whatever, and weekends—I think—all they do is go to birthday parties for other people's kids. I swear. But my brother told me that last weekend, Julie came downstairs and told him he'd have to get rid of the fly-tying table. She's pregnant again—I forgot to mention that. That he'd have to get rid of the table because they need the space for a play area. Now already, Emma's got her dollhouse and stuffed animals and all this other crap down there, and Skip's got his Legos and fifty million Hot Wheels. All Mike has managed is to sort of rope off this little corner to tie flies in. But now she tells him he has to give that up too. And I guess, he told me, he just lost it. He totally lost it and he started yelling at Julie and she started crying, and she was like, "This isn't a mansion." And he was like, "I'm not a pack mule—you treat me like a fucking pack mule." And now, Mike thinks, if he wants to keep his little corner, then basically he's going to have to buy a bigger house. And Julie's an entirely reasonable person. She's not some psycho or something. We used to hang out with them all the time. We used to really have fun with them. For, like, a whole year, all we did was eat at different ethnic restaurants.

KAREN: She puts together scrapbooks?

JASPER: Insanely complicated scrapbooks.

KAREN: Maybe it's relaxing.

JASPER: Again, I'm not down on Julie and it's not, like, with this fiercely contested corner, that Julie beat Mike, or that Mike beat Julie.

[Small beat.]

Or that Melinda will beat me or we'll beat Dan or Dan and Windsong will beat us . . . It's, like, we all got beat. We all got beat way back, way back before the race even started. Before the gun went off. Somebody stole our shoes or severed our hamstrings but we didn't notice. We're just a big bunch of stinking losers who are putting our heads down and running as fast as we can straight into our graves.

[Beat.]

Does that seem harsh?

KAREN: No.

TOM: Not at all.

[KAREN *and* TOM *exchange a look. Then* KAREN *picks up the unopened bottle of wine.*]

KAREN: Would anyone mind if I opened this?

JASPER: No, I was actually—I'm starving.

KAREN: That salad looked good.

TOM: Weren't there some grapes?

KAREN: Over here.

[JASPER *uncovers bowls and gets plates.* KAREN *uncorks the wine and pours. They make a little supper for themselves. For a moment, no one speaks.*]

TOM: I guess I see it differently.

JASPER: You do?

TOM: I've never imagined it as running straight into your grave. I've always seen it as you make a decision and that decision, once planted, sprouts a whole tree of decisions. Like, say, you decided to stay in your hometown. Then that means you go to family gatherings, you join the Masons, you buy your car from the guy you went to high school with who can give you that deal. And then you're sort of borne up, borne along as the tree of that first decision grows until you find yourself precariously perched on the topmost branch, wishing you could get the fuck down.

KAREN: I think of it as a cascade.

TOM: Really?

KAREN: You make the first decision and then it just cascades down from there.

[JASPER, TOM, *and* KAREN *eat.*]

JASPER: You're atheists?

KAREN: We are.

JASPER: For how long?

KAREN: Oh, forever, I guess.

TOM: We don't really talk about it. We learned a long time ago it's an impossible conversation. But if anyone asks we try to be up front.

JASPER: So you're not even agnostic?

TOM: Nope.

[KAREN *shakes her head "no."*]

JASPER: You seem very at peace with it.

TOM: Politics, of course, we try to convert people. Unionizing. I think that's where our proselytizing instincts lie. With something that can actually be of benefit. To people.

KAREN: We don't mind not having any friends, but we'd rather people didn't throw things at us.

JASPER: You don't mind not having friends?

TOM: We have friends, I guess, dinner-party friends. But not *good* friends.

JASPER: How do you define good friends?

TOM: Someone who respects you. Who shares your worldview, your sense of humor. But people are ultimately put off by us. Either it's the kid thing, or the God thing . . .

KAREN: Or our bad personalities.

[*Beat.*]

Even the most liberal, tolerant people still draw lines in the sand. Including us.

JASPER: The Ralph Nader thing was a deal breaker, wasn't it?

KAREN: I'm afraid so. Is this goat cheese? In the salad?

JASPER: I think so. Does it taste like goat cheese?

KAREN: Yes. It's delicious.

TOM: You have to make yourself hard inside, to withstand the world.

[*Beat.*]

KAREN: See, Tom and I, we promised to tell each other the truth, when we got married. We were both divorced before. Did you know that?

JASPER: No.

KAREN: I had been married to a musician, a bass player. At the time, I basically supported the two of us. I was working HR at Sears then, this was . . . 1977, '78. We were living in this really terrible apartment in Rogers Park and I had to wear these hideous suits to work. Gary, my husband, was learning to play rockabilly. He'd bought this stand-up bass and he'd grown his hair out long in front, and long sideburns, and he'd started rolling his own cigarettes—

TOM: This is maybe not to the point.

KAREN: But it is about one thing: He wanted to have children. Even though he didn't have a job. And I was ready to do it, not because I wanted to, but because I'd always assumed I would. When I thought about it, I'd see myself coming home from work and making dinner for the whole family, while Gary sat with his feet up on the table. He had these weird double-jointed toes . . .

[TOM *makes a motion to move* KAREN *along.*]

So when I imagined it, I saw myself as being tired and overwhelmed but never really complaining. That was the important part. I think I was very drawn to an idea of myself as some sort of misunderstood martyr. A person of hidden depths who was never able to live up to her full potential.

TOM: We're always constructing obstacles between ourselves and what we want.

JASPER: Why?

TOM: If there were no obstacles, how else would you explain your failure?

KAREN: That whole time when I was married to Gary, in my head, I had an omniscient narration going on. "Wearily, Karen placed the bag of groceries on the kitchen counter. The dishes from breakfast were still soaking in the sink. Gary sat with his feet up on the coffee table, cracking his weirdly double-jointed toes. She knew there was no one there to hear her."

TOM: And then I came along.

KAREN: We already knew each other, actually. We'd dated in college.

JASPER: Really?

TOM: Senior year. But it didn't work out.

KAREN: We liked each other too much.

JASPER: What?

KAREN: See—I thought relationships had to be very, very hard because my parents' marriage was such a disaster. I'd never really been around a couple who liked each other—

TOM: Me neither. And Karen and I really did. We liked each other. We had fun together. I thought she was smart and funny and so pretty.

KAREN: And I thought Tom was great. Just, really, so handsome. But he treated me well.

TOM: And she didn't make me feel like shit all the time.

KAREN: It was so outside our frame of reference, it made us nervous. So we broke up. I went to Berkeley for graduate school.

TOM: And I went to Case Western and I met this woman, Andrea. I got my degree and this job offer in Chicago. I asked Andrea if she wanted to come along, and we could live together. But she didn't want to do that, because her father was a Lutheran minister and she didn't want to upset him by living in sin. So I said, "Well, then do you want to get married?" And she said yes. I didn't think that through, maybe.

JASPER: Maybe not.

TOM: We had a huge wedding and then in the limousine, on the way to the reception, Andrea starting crying. She said it was because her flowers were wilting.

[*Beat.*]

The only apartment we could afford in Chicago was right next to a homeless shelter. She lasted a year before she said she just couldn't take it anymore and she had to get back to Chagrin Falls.

KAREN: Lovely town.

TOM: So I was newly divorced and working in the mayor's office and Jimmy Carter was running against Ronald Reagan. And somebody put a list of people on my desk who had volunteered to campaign, and I saw this name, Karen Whitaker. And I thought, "Could it be?"

KAREN: He had called me once, in Berkeley.

TOM: I just said hi.

KAREN: I was married already. It was awkward.

TOM: I called her right after Andrea and I got engaged. I didn't want to tell her that. But I think I wanted to find out, before I walked down the aisle, was there some chance . . . ?

JASPER: Wow.

KAREN: And I didn't tell him that I kept this old picture of him. It was in a drawer in my desk at work. Under some envelopes. Where I could always find it.

[Beat.]

JASPER: So her name was on the list . . .

TOM: Yes, and I thought, "My God, what if this is her?" And I called the number and she answered.

KAREN: I was really happy to hear his voice.

TOM: But she was still married.

KAREN: But I thought, "There's no harm in getting a drink together. So he's an old boyfriend, so what?"

TOM: We went out on a Sunday afternoon because somehow a Sunday afternoon seemed very up front.

KAREN: He looked so great.

TOM: She looked gorgeous. And she was still as smart and as warm as I remembered. With that heart.

KAREN: Your heart.

[*Beat.*]

We started seeing each other around the election. We'd work phone banks together and then go get a drink. Gary had actually gotten a gig with this rockabilly band in Madison and he was driving back and forth, so I didn't really have to explain where I was. And then one night we didn't even work the banks, we just went to this Italian restaurant and then over to the Green Mill—

TOM: It was near my apartment. And I asked her, "What do you want to do? Do you want to get a divorce?"

KAREN: And I said yes. I hadn't said it out loud before.

TOM: And she came back to my place and we committed adultery.

KAREN: It was awful.

[*Pause.*]

I had always, before that, been very firm on policy. People who cheated on their spouses were terrible people. I went back home, early in the morning, and got in bed and stayed there. I was sick. I was hungover. I was guilty. The sex hadn't even been that good.

TOM: In college it had been great. I thought.

KAREN: Me too. But this hadn't been great. It had been sort of terrifying.

[*Beat.*]

Gary was coming home from Madison that night, and I knew I had to tell him something because I was so guilty I couldn't stand being in the same room with him. So when he came in, I told him I'd been thinking while he was gone, and that I was very unhappy and I wanted a divorce. And Gary started crying because to him it came from out of nowhere. But the next morning he got up and packed his things and went to live with his uncle.

TOM: But then we didn't know what to do.

KAREN: Tom thought maybe I was just using him because I was afraid of being alone and I thought he'd get tired of me and start dating other women, and that went on for a while . . .

TOM: Six months or so. But we kept calling each other. I'd call her from work in the middle of the day with some dumb question.

KAREN: One night we went to another Italian restaurant and I remember I looked at him and said something to the effect that all this wrangling was ridiculous. That I had always wanted to be with him. This was now . . . almost ten years since we'd dated in college—

JASPER: Really?

KAREN: Yes.

TOM: And I'd always wanted to be with her. And what were we doing? Just being stupid again? Because why? Because neither of us deserved to be happy? Why not? Why couldn't we be happy?

KAREN: The worst thing I ever did was cheat on Gary. I'm not proud of it, but it's the worst thing I ever did. We weren't terrible people. Couldn't we be happy?

[Beat.]

I remember after we left the restaurant, when we were waiting for the train, we were sitting on one of those nasty benches on the platform . . .

[KAREN *trails off for a moment.*]

And Tom put his arm around me.

[*Long pause.*]

And we promised each other two things: that we would never lie to each other and that we would never get married.

JASPER: Why? That you would never get married? Why that?

TOM: That seemed like the highest accolade then because we both thought you only married people you hated.

KAREN: We didn't want to fall into anything again.

TOM: So we lived together for eight years. Then one morning, Karen proposed.

KAREN: We were going to buy this place. It seemed to make sense. And it was April.

TOM: I wasn't surprised.

KAREN: So we went down to the courthouse and there was a huge long line, because it was a Saturday.

TOM: You don't need a witness it turns out.

KAREN: The ceremony took three minutes.

TOM: And we were hitched. Then we came home, and we both went for a run along the lake and I remember feeling so elated. I wasn't expecting it exactly. But I felt so free and so bound at the same time. So set.

KAREN: It felt like there was an extra allotment of oxygen in the air.

[*Beat.*]

It was because we did it and we didn't tell anyone. So you could never say that we'd done it for anyone else. We'd done it entirely for ourselves.

[*Pause.*]

Sometimes I wonder if we protest too much. If we have to keep saying we love each other because we depend on each other so much, so if we fell out of love that would truly be a disaster. But then I think, "How could we depend on each other so much if we didn't love each other?" And I think, "What, exactly, is wrong with being in love?"

TOM: It's not that we didn't want to share that with a child. It's that we've never felt the need for a child. Is the real reason.

[*Beat.*]

JASPER: Because baby makes three.

[TOM *and* KAREN *both look at him.* JASPER *looks at nothing. Pause.*]

KAREN: We'll help you carry all this inside.

JASPER: It's okay. Really.

TOM: You sure?

JASPER: Yeah. Guys. Yeah. This was great.

TOM [*to* KAREN]: You still want to go see the fireworks?

KAREN: I do.

TOM [to JASPER]: Tell Melinda good night for us.

JASPER: I will.

[TOM opens the gate for KAREN.]

KAREN: 'Night, Jasper.

JASPER: Good night.

[TOM and KAREN exit. Pause. JASPER stares ahead. The back door opens and MELINDA comes out onto the porch. She's wearing pajama-type pants and a T-shirt. She looks great. She stands on the porch.]

MELINDA: Jasper?

JASPER: Huh? Hey. What—

[JASPER looks around.]

I kind of got sidetracked.

MELINDA: Were Tom and Karen out here?

JASPER: We had something to eat after all.

MELINDA: What'd they want?

JASPER: To apologize for—they said they're sorry if they drove everybody away. That Dan seems funny. And Windsong seems sweet.

MELINDA: That was nice.

JASPER: Yeah.

[Beat.]

They were talking about weddings.

MELINDA: I'm sorry we laughed about that picture.

JASPER: It hurts my feelings. When you laugh at me.

MELINDA: We were just kidding.

[*Pause.*]

JASPER: What'd we do after our wedding? I can't remember.

MELINDA: My mom and dad got us that honeymoon suite, at the Fairmont.

JASPER: Right.

MELINDA: We were supposed to get a champagne dinner but we got there too late.

JASPER: And they gave us that key, a real key, and I thought it was to a safe or the minibar or something, so when we checked out I gave it back. But it was engraved, remember? With the room number and the date. We were supposed to keep it as a souvenir. I've always felt bad about that.

MELINDA: I think my mom called and got a partial refund. For the dinner.

[*Beat.*]

JASPER: At the reception—remember Dwight pushed Dan in the pool?

MELINDA: Yes.

JASPER: I think everybody we knew was there.

MELINDA: There were a lot of people.

JASPER: I remember cutting the cake and looking around, thinking, "How is this cake going to feed all these people?"

MELINDA: We should have had a groom's cake.

JASPER: Thinking all these people came just to watch us eat cake.

MELINDA: They came to watch us get married.

JASPER: Just to watch us get married.

[*Pause.*]

MELINDA: I couldn't find a good movie—

JASPER [*quickly*]: I don't want to do it.

MELINDA: What?

JASPER: I really—I don't want to do it.

[MELINDA *stares at him.*]

Tell me it's okay. Tell me we'll still be happy together. Tell me we love each other enough not to have to have a baby.

[MELINDA *doesn't answer.*]

Please?

MELINDA: Fuck you. I am so sick of your shit.

[MELINDA *turns and starts inside.*]

JASPER: Melinda. . . !

MELINDA: No "Melinda." Fuck you!

[MELINDA *goes inside and slams the door hard behind her.* JASPER *looks after her. He looks around the backyard. Then he goes to a chair and sits. Pause. He picks up a beer that could have belonged to anyone and takes a swig. Pause.*]

JASPER [*quietly*]: Jasper sat, alone, in the growing darkness. He looked at the remains of a party gone horribly awry. "I should go after her," he thought to himself.

[JASPER *drinks.*]

"I should really go in after her."

[JASPER *doesn't move. Lights fade.*]

Dan (Kiff Vanden Heuvel) does his imitation of Jasper as "robot-boy" for Windsong (Stephanie Childers, left) and Melinda (Janelle Snow).

Jasper (Coburn Goss) reassures Melinda (Snow) that they will have a family in due time.

Dwight (Sean Cooper, right) tells Tom (Rob Riley) that he is "totally cool."

Karen (Linda Gehringer) and Tom (Riley) tell their side of the story.